# ALEXA, GET ME A MORTGAGE

**ALEXA RAE FAITHFUL (NMLS #1465347)**
706-338-5073
alexa@cmsmortgage.com
1612 Centerville Turnpike, Suite 307
Virginia Beach, VA 23464
Equal Housing Lender

To the best of our knowledge, the information contained herein is accurate and reliable as of the date of publication; however, we do not assume any liability whatsoever for the accuracy and completeness of the below information.

Any information given in this book should not be mistaken for legal advice. It is the customers' responsibility to determine which mortgage program would suit your needs the best.

"*I never truly understood the meaning of warmth until I purchased my own home. As I sit in my own living room, surrounded by walls painted my favorite color, looking out at the mighty oak tree sitting on the lot I so carefully chose and listening to the tranquil sounds of my jazz music on the stereo, my soul is filled with deep contentment, a warmth that I could not before have imagined.*"

–**Anonymous**

*This book is dedicated to my incredible husband, Drew and our hilarious son, Elias. You both are my greatest treasures and the reason for all I do.*

**—Alexa**

# TABLE OF CONTENTS

Introduction ................................................................ xi

1. Choosing The Right Style of Home ........................................ 1

2. Things To Consider Before Deciding On A Property ......... 4

3. Special Financing Programs ................................................ 6

4. When You Know, You Know ................................................ 9

5. Real Estate Agents ............................................................ 11

6. The Pre-Approval ............................................................. 13

7. Understand The Home Buying Process Before You Start ................................................................................... 15

8. Keep An Open Mind ........................................................ 23

9. Choose An Agent That You Like ...................................... 25

10. Leave Your Money Alone ................................................ 27

11. Where To Find The Right Lender ................................... 29

12. Get To Know Your Future Neighborhood Better ........... 31

13. Write A Love Letter ........................................................ 33

14. Auction & Bank Owned Properties ................................ 35

15. What Credit Score Do I Need To Get A Mortgage? ......... 36

16. What Will You Look At When I Apply For A Mortgage? ................................................................................ 38

17. What Does It Mean To Pre-Qualify For A Home Loan? ....................................................................................... 40

18. Minimum Down Payments ................................................. 42

19. Out Of Pocket Costs ............................................................ 44

20. Should I Pay Discount Points? .......................................... 45

21. The Difference Between A Fixed-Rate Mortgage And ARM Loan .............................................................................. 47

22. What Will My Mortgage Payment Include? .................... 49

23. Can Someone Give Me Money For My Down Payment? ................................................................................ 50

24. Owning V. Renting .............................................................. 51

25. How Long Does It Take To Buy A House? ...................... 53

26. What Is An Earnest Money Deposit? ................................ 54

27. Is There A Loan Program That Allows Me To Fix Up A House In Need Of Repairs? ............................................ 55

28. Is There A Difference Between Buying A Home To Live In And Buying An Investment Property? .......................... 57

29. Four Questions To Ask When Buying A Flip ................. 59

30. Condos Are An Affordable Path To Homeownership ... 62

31. What Are Contingencies? ........................................................ 65

32. Explore Your Down Payment Options .............................. 68

33. Let's Talk About Sewers ........................................................ 72

34. Attention Military - Top 5 Reasons You Want To Use Your VA Loan Benefit ............................................................ 75

35. 15 Year Mortgage vs 30 Year Mortgage ............................. 78

36. More Money Down Or Nah? ............................................... 82

37. Do You Like To Gamble? ...................................................... 85

38. How Can I Best Be Prepared To Get A Home Loan ........ 89

39. Conclusion ............................................................................... 94

# INTRODUCTION

If you're reading this book, it's probably not because you were bored and had nothing better to do, and more likely because you are thinking about purchasing a home. We will cover everything you'll need to know plus some, but first a little ditty about me and how it ultimately led to the creation of this book.

I have been in the mortgage and personal finance space for five years. My decision to get into the mortgage industry was very much a result of my own experience purchasing my first home.

Much like many first time home buyers, I was young, broke, had a credit score that was less than impressive, and didn't know the first thing about buying Real Estate. As much as I tried to rely on the internet for answers, it seemed each website had conflicting information, and I couldn't find a Loan Officer that was willing to tell me what I needed to do to qualify.

When I finally did take the first step in applying for a pre-approval, I was denied and told that I needed to wait. Wait? For what? Needless to say, I grew frustrated at the lack of feedback and clarity. But I simply couldn't shake the desire to own my own home. So I persisted.

I finally got connected with the right person who told me exactly what I needed to do to qualify. Turns out, it wasn't nearly as daunting as I thought it would be.

About 3 months later, I found myself signing the closing papers on my very first home. It was unlike any feeling I have ever experienced before. That moment was the catalyst that changed my personal and financial trajectory of my life.

I knew that I couldn't be the only one who had the desire to achieve their goal of owning property, and I knew there had to be a better way to educate homebuyers with the right information.

I decided that I would be the better way. Since then, I have dedicated my career to helping people in all walks of life obtain their goals of home ownership.

I do this through not only continuing my own education, but by taking extra time with each client to get to know more than just their credit score and level of income. I want to know what matters to them. What drives them. What their daily lifestyle looks like. I want to know what their future looks like. By gaining this information with each client, I'm able to connect them to the product that best aligns with their personal goals and objectives.

The home is the epicenter of our lives. It's the place that we grow, change, and reside in throughout all the varying seasons of our life. So the decision to make something that special your own is not one that should be made lightly or without a thorough understanding of all it entails.

I hope this book serves as a resource to assist you in what will be one of the most important financial transactions you will ever make.

Ready to dive in? Lessgo!

Alexa Rae Faithful

# 1

# Choosing The Right Style of Home

When you're a first time homebuyer and you're finally ready to say peace out to the rental life, it's helpful to know the different types of properties that exist and the pros and cons of owning each.

There are four main types of properties.

## Single Family Home

The first is a single family home. Picture a typical suburban neighborhood. Single Family Homes are detached from other homes, often with an attached OR detached garage and space in between each property.

This is the most common type of home purchased in America.

It's the kind of place that people will envision when they think about the American Dream. But it is not the only type of property. While a SFH offers space and privacy, it can also mean more maintenance, so that is something you'll need to keep in mind when deciding what style of home is right for you.

There are other types of homes that work for different types of people as well.

## Condos

Another popular property type is a Condo. A Condo is similar to an apartment but instead of a property management company owning the entire building, each unit is owned by an individual.

In a condo, you own everything inside your walls. Everything outside your walls is either common space, owned by somebody else, or belongs to the complex itself.

Condos are great if you're looking for a home with low maintenance and lots of amenities. However, Condos are managed by companies known as Homeowner Associations, which require either monthly or annual fees called homeowner association dues as well as a list of rules that residents in the community must abide by.

These fees will cover things like your amenities, taking care of the parking lots, security, and lawn care.

Condos are ideal for folks who don't want the upkeep that comes with a SFH but still want to own their place.

## Townhomes

The third type of property is a townhome.

A townhome is similar to a condo in that you have shared walls but with a townhome, you own everything inside of your unit as well as the front and back of it.

You might have a little more property on the outside of your unit with a townhome like a small deck or yard.

Occasionally, you will see townhome complexes that also have garages or additional storage space that you typically don't get with a condo.

## Duplex

The fourth type of property is a duplex.

A duplex is a unit that includes two completely separate homes that are attached in the middle.

Typically if you own a duplex, you're going to own the entire unit. In some areas you may be able to buy only one half of the duplex, although this is rare. If possible, always opt to own the entire unit.

Duplexes provide an enormous opportunity for passive income as you can live in one unit and rent out the other (assuming you own the entire unit which is most common). Then when you are ready to move onto the next property down the road, you can opt to keep the duplex and rent out both units... Hello rental income! It's like buying an investment property without having to put 20% down. This strategy is also known as "house hacking" as you are leveraging the property type to provide passive income.

In a Duplex, you own everything inside and outside your unit as well as both front and back yard spaces.

# 2

# Things To Consider Before Deciding On A Property

Now that you understand the different types of homes that are out there, it's really important to know and read the fine print so to speak, before you buy into any given neighborhood... Particularly one with a Homeowners Association (HOA). Every HOA is a little bit different in what they allow and what they don't allow.

Each neighborhood association will also have different requirements of the homeowners as well as different association dues. So if you're the artistic type that values expressing yourself with a bright pink door, you'll want to double check to ensure things like that are permitted in the community bylaws before making an offer. But creativity isn't the only thing that might or might not be limited in a neighborhood with an HOA.

Let's say for example you own a camper or an RV and it's important to you to be able to park it at your house. You want to read the HOA documents to make sure that's an option as many associations have restrictions on what types of things you can have on your physical property.

If that's not possible you can review the documents during your inspection period. You will have the ability to get out of the contract during the inspection period if you find something in the HOA docs that you know won't jive with your lifestyle.

# 3

# Special Financing Programs

The most important thing you can do BEFORE you start shopping for homes is to speak to a Mortgage Lender and to get pre-approved. (We'll dive deeper into this process later).

It's essential that you talk to a mortgage professional first so that you can know exactly which mortgage programs you qualify for and how much home you can afford.

In the event that you qualify for more than one program, understanding the difference in each will set you up to make the best choice that will align with your short and long term financial goals.

There are some special government programs that make it easier for renters to become homeowners or for people to move up into new homes.

Let's explore some different government loan programs beginning with the **VA Loan Program**.

VA stands for Veterans Administration. This is a loan that is available for most Veterans and active duty military.

There are some requirements for the amount of time you have to have served, and this will depend on branch and status. So even if you have served or are currently serving, you'll want to speak with a Loan Officer to make sure that you do qualify. They can also pull a document known as a Certificate of Eligibility from the VA which confirms if you qualify or not.

The best part about the VA loan is that there is no down payment required. It actually covers 100% of your loan amount. The interest rates are also among the lowest out there which makes it a pretty sweet deal all around for those who qualify.

Another type of special program is the **FHA Program**.

This was designed for homebuyers with low to median income that are limited in how much cash they can bring to the closing table.

In most cases, the FHA program only requires a 3.5% down payment compared to a normal conventional home loan that requires 5% to 20% down.

The third government program that helps home buyers get into a house with little to no money out of pocket is the **USDA Program**. If you like country living, the USDA program might be an excellent option.

The US Department of Agriculture (the same folks who approve your meats in the grocery store) also have a loan program!

This program is particularly awesome for low to median income buyers because it also does not require a downpayment and provides 100% financing.

While the USDA loan is great for certain folks, it also has its own caveats and requirements. For example, the property has to be located in an area that is deemed "rural". You can search specific property addresses on their eligibility map by Google searching "USDA loan eligibility map".

The USDA also has caps on total household income. The income limits include ALL household members, which include household members that are not on the loan itself. So be sure to provide your Loan Officer with your pay stubs, W2's and tax returns of every wage earner in the house to ensure you fall within the income limits of this program.

In addition to nationwide government programs, there might also be **local grants** available depending on which state you live in.

In some cases, those grants will cover a portion of your down payment and/or closing costs.

It's important to remember that the guidelines to these programs can change pretty quickly. And grant funds are often limited and can run out quickly.

You'll want to speak with a local professional to find out if you qualify for any grant programs that currently exist.

# 4

# When You Know, You Know

When you find a home that gives you all of those warm & fuzzy feelings and meets enough of your criteria, acting quickly is crucial.

Depending on the market, there is a good chance you will encounter some friendly (or not so friendly) competition from other buyers looking to make an offer on the same home.

The market at the time this book was written is the most aggressive we have seen in years. Due to low inventory, low rates, and high demand, It is a textbook seller's market so the competition is stiff.

Many buyers are competing with other buyers to the point of having to go above the asking price of the property in order to win the deal.

This is another reason it is so important to have a pre-approval BEFORE you are ready to start hunting and making offers. At this stage, there should be no reason to wait in getting your offer in as fast as possible. So when you know, be ready to bring your A-game.

When a seller receives an offer from a buyer they have three options in what they can do:

## 1. They can accept the offer

They can take your offer exactly the way that it has been presented and execute or ratify the contract. If this happens, congratulations! You've accomplished something rare in the world of real estate negotiations.

## 2. They can do nothing

The seller can receive your offer and do nothing nor offer any response. This is not typical however, aside from just being downright impolite, there's no legal requirement for them to respond to your offer.

## 3. They can counter your offer

If your offer is not immediately accepted or blatantly rejected by the seller, the most common move is for them to make a counter offer.

If they do counter, it could be based on purchase price or on other pieces of the contract, such as the earnest money deposit, the amount of your closing costs that they're willing to pay, the closing date, the inspection period, and things of that nature.

So again, when you find a house that you're interested in that you feel could be a good fit for you and your family, acting swiftly is crucial.

# 5

# Real Estate Agents

Firstly, Real Estate Agents are different from Realtors. A Realtor is a trademarked term that refers to Agents that are an active part of a National Association of Realtors (NAR). But for purposes of this book, I'll use both titles interchangeably.

It's a common misconception that the buyer is the one to pay their Real Estate Agent to represent them. Although the buyer's agent does get paid, they are paid by the seller's Real Estate Agent (often referred to as the Listing Agent), not the buyer.

When a person lists their home for sale, they sign a listing agreement with an agent of their choice.

The listing agreement will cover things like the price at which the home will be listed, how long they are going to work together, as well as what their commission will be should they succeed in selling their client's home.

So, let's say for example, the seller agrees to pay 6% towards total Realtor commissions. The listing agent technically gets to decide how to split the commission. They usually keep 3% and offer 3% to the agent who represents the buyer. This is among the most common commission structures, but can vary based on your individual market.

# 6

# The Pre-Approval

The first true step in the home purchase process is the pre-approval. This is sometimes referred to as a pre-qualification. We'll dive a bit deeper into the subtle differences in being pre-approved vs. being pre-qualified a little later in the book. But for now, let's cover the overview of the pre-approval.

This is arguably the most important part in the home buying process. Everything hinges on this. I can't stress this enough.

One of the worst feelings is to go and find the home of your dreams, put in an offer that's accepted by the seller, only to find out a few weeks later that you don't qualify for one reason or another. Don't put yourself at risk for that level of heartbreak... Your Agent will thank you for it too.

I could probably write a whole second book on the things that can jeopardize a pre-approval. It can range from income, assets, changes in your employment or hours, or even something as subtle as how you have your student loan payments set up. Throw in something like, oh I don't know, a Pandemic, and things have real potential to get sticky.

Being pre-approved means knowing exactly what loan programs you qualify for as well as how much house you qualify for. This is done by completing an application with a local Mortgage Lender.

Another benefit of being pre-approved prior to shopping is identifying any red flags that might trip you up during the loan process, and resolving them before you are actually under contract.

Your Loan Officer will review your application, credit report, tax returns, W2's, pay stubs, bank statements, and other personal documents to let you know if there are any potential issues that you will need to be aware of and resolve prior to making any offers.

Prepare yourself for this stage in the process because it can and will feel like... a lot. The Loan approval process doesn't rank very high on the "FUN list" of life activities.

Just when you think you've provided every possible personal document to your Loan Officer, the Underwriter will find something else that they need from you. It's not your chronic bad luck striking again. It's simply par for the course. You're borrowing hundreds of thousands of dollars over the course of three decades, so Lenders have to fully vet each and every buyer to ensure they aren't setting them up for failure and that they possess the ability to repay the loan.

Just remember, your Loan Officer is your friend and they are here to help you.

The pre-approval provides the confidence you need to ensure that the home you're making an offer on is one that you will qualify for.

# 7

# Understand The Home Buying Process Before You Start

One of the most overwhelming parts of purchasing a home is understanding the process from start to finish. To help with streamlining your understanding of the process, I've boiled it down to seven basic steps.

These steps will help you in always knowing where you are at any given point once you begin your home buying journey.

**Step 1. Get Pre-Approved**

I know what you're thinking... 'Alright, Alexa. We get it!' We just talked about how important it is to get pre-approved so you will know exactly how much home you're qualified for and what your payment will be on that house. But having a full pre-approval also provides the seller with confidence knowing that they are working with a buyer that will actually close.

Got it? Cool... Moving on...

## Step 2. Find The Right Agent Who Will Find The Right House

Next, you're going to hire a Real Estate Agent who will help you in finding the perfect home that will meet your needs and align with your budget.

Your Realtor has access to the MLS (Multiple Listing System), which offers them details on every home on the market including houses that you might not be able to find on Zillow, Realtor.com or any other websites. These are sometimes called "pocket listings" or "off market listings"

When choosing an Agent, you want to be sure you're working with someone you feel you can trust. It's always good to ask for referrals from friends or family members that have recently bought a home. Ask them what they liked about their Agent, or if not, what things could have made their experience better. This will help you choose an Agent that will provide you with top notch service from start to finish.

Your Agent might require you to sign a "buyer brokerage agreement" which essentially means you can't drag them around to show you 25 different homes and then decide to use another agent at the drop of a hat. This is to protect their time and expertise, and also helps solidify the professional relationship you'll build with them throughout the process.

## Step 3. Write An Offer and Ratify The Contract

So you found the house of your dreams! *dance break* Now it's time to work with your Agent to prepare your written offer to the sellers.

At this point, you are offering to enter a formal sales contract with the seller, but it's only signed by you. The seller will choose to sign as is our counter once they review the offer.

On the offer contract, it will include the price, what loan program you'll be using, when you want to close, how much money you want to put up as a down payment, and all the other parts of your offer such as how much of your closing costs you want the seller to pay, if any.

Once the seller accepts and signs the written offer, you're officially under a ratified contract! *cue second dance break*

## Step 4. Get a Home Inspection

Once you're under contract, you usually have a specified period of time by which you must order and schedule the home inspection.

The role of the Home Inspector is to go through the property with a fine tooth comb to identify any structural or cosmetic issues or defects that might have potential to cause issues regarding the safety or integrity of the property.

Your home inspector is going to be an independent but licensed individual who probably has never been in the house before.

They will have a checklist and it will likely take them several hours to complete the full inspection.

The home inspector at the end might even invite you to the house so that they can go over what they have found. They also provide a written report.

Understand that it's the inspector's job to point out everything that's wrong or damaged in the home, but each imperfection they point out will not necessarily mean that it's a bad idea to proceed with the purchase.

Once you review the home inspection, you'll have an opportunity to request that the sellers make certain repairs. You'll want to be very calculated in what you ask of the sellers.

While you're going-over that report, it's important to know what's important and what's not. What is a deal breaker and what's not?

What can you ask the sellers to repair and what could you repair yourself after you move in?

One suggestion is never to ask the seller to repair every item on the inspection checklist. You want to show that you are reasonable and you're not going to ask them to repair the small things that aren't that important or super costly, especially if it's something that you could easily do yourself when you move in.

The repairs that the sellers agree to will be noted on a document referred to as the PICRA (Property Inspection Contingency Removal Addendum).

## Step 5. The Home Appraisal

The next step is to order the appraisal. Your Lender is responsible for ordering the appraisal. At this stage, the appraisal company will assign a local licensed appraiser to go out and determine the current market value of the home.

The value of the home is determined by not only the condition of the subject property, but is also based on comparable properties in the nearby area that have sold within the past 12 months or so. The appraiser will compare the subject property to these comparable properties (also referred to as "comps"), to determine the current market value.

There are several potential outcomes of an appraisal. The first is the value will either be at least what you have agreed to pay for it or higher. If this is the case, your lender will give it the stamp of approval, and you can proceed with the next step in the process.

However, sometimes the appraisal will determine that the home is worth the agreed upon purchase price, IF AND ONLY IF certain repairs are made. When this happens, the value is *contingent* on the repairs which must be made in order for the Lender to approve the loan.

In this scenario, the seller will need to agree to make the specified repairs, and then have the appraiser come back out to the property for a "final inspection" to ensure the work has been done up to code.

If for some reason the home comes in at a lower value than what you have agreed to pay, you'll either need to renegotiate the contract or you'll have to pay the difference out-of-pocket.

In summary, the purpose of the appraisal is to protect you, the buyer, from paying more than what the home is worth. It also protects the bank from lending more than what the home is valued at.

## Step 6. Receive Full Loan Approval

Once the home inspection and appraisal report check out, it's time to keep chugging along in your loan approval.

At this stage, your Loan Officer will submit all of your loan documents to an Underwriter for review. The Underwriter will review all of your income, assets, and credit report to ensure it meets the criteria for the loan program you have chosen. Some Lenders also have their own specific criteria that must be met in order to receive approval. These are known as Lender Overlays.

After review, the Underwriter might come back (and when I say **might** come back, I really mean **WILL**) and ask for a handful of missing documents, or explanations for certain things like discrepancies in addresses on your documents or a myriad of other personal situations that will vary from person to person. This stage is known as "conditional approval".

At this point in the process, it can be tempting to feel like you're having to provide all but your first born's left ear. I often hear "what I have provided SHOULD be sufficient"... And maybe you're right. But you're also not an Underwriter, and I'm not either. Mainly because I like smiling and I don't dig ruining people's day.

Keep in mind that your Loan Officer doesn't write the loan guidelines, but they do have to follow them. It often pains us just as much to ask for more documents as it pains you to provide them.

If and when you begin to feel frustrated in the process, take a deep breath and think about what it will feel like to be handed the keys to your very own home. Holding this vision close will ease the pain points that will inevitably pop up throughout your home buying journey.

Once you provide the Underwriter with all remaining documentation, he or she will grant final approval and clear to close! *cue mini confetti cannons and tears of joy*

## Step 7. Sign Closing Papers And Get The Keys

Now that you have received final approval, the Lender will work with the Title company to collaborate on final figures and you will be issued a preliminary closing disclosure to sign. It's customary for the initial closing disclosure to still be an estimate and will almost never be finalized the first time around. But always sign this immediately, as final figures will be balanced upon signing the initial closing disclosure.

There is also a mandatory three business day waiting period that has to elapse before you can close. That waiting period begins only after signing the preliminary closing disclosure. So be sure to not dilly-dally in signing that sucker ASAP.

From there, the closing documents are sent in one big electronic package to the Title company. Your closing agent will usually reach out to you to schedule a closing date and time.

Now comes the best part… CLOSING DAY! Crank up that power song you've been saving for this day!

On closing day, you'll meet with your Title agent and Realtor at the Title company (or another specified location) to sign all of the closing documents. Most of the documents you will have reviewed and or signed once prior to this point, but your Title Agent will explain everything to you once more.

After signing everything, you'll be handed the keys to your very own home. You did it! You are a HOMEOWNER! *cue fireworks and emotional celebration montage*

# 8
# Keep An Open Mind

Now that we've covered an overview of the process, let's dive deeper into a few more things you'll want to know.

The home buying process can be an exciting and empowering experience. However, it's very important to keep a level head and an open mind. It's easy for emotions to take over, and when that happens, you're less likely to adhere to reality in terms of your budget and what you can afford.

A $100,000 budget looks different from a $300,000 budget... This seems glaringly obvious, right? But where people go wrong is to start looking "just for fun" at homes that are outside of their price point. Doing so will only set yourself up for heartache and house envy, which are lame feelings.

There is no right budget or wrong budget. There is only *your* budget. So make your budget work for you. If you find that you have exhausted the available homes in your area that fall within your budget, you can also ask your Loan Officer if adding a co-signer to the loan is an option. Some loan programs allow this, others don't.

One exercise that can be helpful is to-do a needs versus wants sheet side-by-side. Take a piece of paper and make one column for needs and one column for wants.

List out things like the bedrooms, bathrooms, different features and layouts, and neighborhoods. Basically all the elements that you feel are important in your future home.

Be honest with yourself in identifying and labeling a true need versus a want.

If you have a large family, 4 bedrooms might be a need. If you are single or married with no children, a three car garage might be a want. Only you will be able to determine what falls into each category.

Also, ye be warned about the 'HGTV Effect'.

Popular home buying and home renovation shows romanticize the home purchase process and can set unrealistic expectations for what your experience might look like. Additionally, a $200,000 home in Muncie Indiana isn't going to look anything like a $200,000 home in Los Angeles. That's assuming you can even FIND a $200,000 home in Los Angeles. Is that even a thing?

Share your needs and wants list with your Agent and have a discussion so you are both on the same page about what elements in a property are going to take priority.

# 9

# Choose An Agent That You Like

Obviously you don't want to work with someone you're not particularly thrilled about, but there is also a lot of trust involved when you are purchasing a home.

You should choose an agent that you enjoy working with that you also feel you can trust. Just because your Mom's yoga teacher's daughter is a licensed Real Estate Agent, doesn't mean that they will be the right agent for you.

You're going to spend a lot of time together, so pick somebody whose company you enjoy and who you feel you can communicate with in a comfortable and effective way.

Find somebody that you feel is going to look out for your best interest and represent you well.

Don't always use the first agent you come across unless you feel a connection with them. Take some time and ask for referrals.

You can even ask your Loan Officer for some referrals since they will know many of the best agents in the local community.

Finding a Realtor you really vibe with and that you want to work with in such an important transaction.

# 10

# Leave Your Money Alone

Lenders have very specific requirements for what can and can't be counted towards your total qualifying assets. There are rules to ensure that the money going into the mortgage and banking system is legitimate and not illegally sourced (Ozark anyone?).

With this in mind, a good rule of thumb is to let your money be. If you have money in the mattress or in a shoebox, you'll want to get that money in the bank at least 3-6 months prior to beginning the home purchase process. Otherwise, your Lender will not be able to count large cash deposits towards funds being used for down payment and closing costs without an explanation and supporting documentation. Especially if they can see the deposits took place in the most recent 60 day period.

In banking, we call the length of time your money needs to be in the account the "seasoning period" and you're going to have to season that money if you want to use it for a down payment or anything that has to do with purchasing a home.

If the money is not seasoned, the mortgage company will definitely ask you to prove where it came from by providing a paper trail that tracks the deposit back to its original source.

They do not want to see any large deposits into your account that aren't easily traceable.

This of course doesn't include your normal paychecks, child support, or any other money you receive on a monthly basis. But more so, large deposits such as random checks or cash that are harder to explain. (Child support and/or alimony payments have their own set of rules and usually require associated documentation such as a court order, divorce decree, or other signed agreement as well as proof of consistent payments having been made over the last 6-12 consecutive months.)

Your Lender will review your most recent two months worth of bank statements for all accounts at the beginning of the process, and then sometimes again at the end to ensure nothing out of the ordinary has transpired with your assets.

So, if you come into any money, don't deposit it into your checking account right before closing without checking with your Loan Officer first. Making any large or unusual moves in your assets could jeopardize your loan approval big time.

# 11

# Where To Find The Right Lender

Generally speaking, most folks start the home buying process online. In today's digital age, it's simply too easy and convenient to pop a few key words into a search bar and receive more results than you could ever need.

But with more options comes a larger chance of inaccurate or outdated information.

It's ok to use online resources for general information gathering purposes, but in the end, you want to find a local professional to help you understand that information and how it pertains to you exactly.

The same holds true for finding your actual home.

Start online with your home search but ultimately you want to find a local Real Estate Agent that you trust and work with them. Remember, just because Uncle Kenny has his Real Estate license, doesn't necessarily mean he's going to be the best option.

Realtors will also have relationships with other agents and this can help you find homes that may not be listed online.

Knowing and working with a local trusted professional will also assist you in the offer stage if your Realtor has relationships with other local agents and homeowners in the area.

# 12

# Get To Know Your Future Neighborhood Better

The neighborhood in which you purchase a home is a big factor to consider outside of just the physical home.

Like many things in life, you can't always judge a neighborhood by the "look" or by a stereotype that you or someone else has assigned to an area. Especially if it's not based on the right factors.

Each neighborhood will have it's own unique vibe and culture.

When possible, try to visit the neighborhood during different times of the day as well as again in the evening to see if there is anything that is worth noticing.

What is it like when everybody is home from work and school?

What are the neighborhood demographics?

Who do you see in the neighborhood?

Are there kids playing?

Are there people walking in the neighborhood or out engaging with other people?

What is it like in the evening time?

It's also a great idea to go to the property on the weekend to see what it's like.

What are people doing in that area? Do the neighbors wave or initiate conversation with you or with each other?

You will get a real feel for the neighborhood by visiting a property during the daytime, evening time, weekday, and weekend.

# 13

# Write A Love Letter

You might be thinking "what on earth does writing a love letter have to do with the purchase process?" Hear me out... Don't worry, it's not about to get weird.

Similarly to finding a romantic partner, finding the right home is something that is accomplished through intentional pursuit.

In this case, I'm talking about writing a letter to the seller of the home you want to purchase, telling them what you love most about the house and a little bit about why you feel it would be perfect for you and your family.

This letter should be no more than one page long and should include how you envision your family living in the house. Bonus points if it's handwritten.

You want to share things like what excites you about the neighborhood and property and why you want this transaction to move forward.

This is a great thing to include with an offer especially when you find yourself in a multiple offer situation.

I once had a client whose offer was accepted against other offers because of the letter that they wrote to the sellers. Their offer wasn't even the highest, but it struck a chord with the sellers who were emotional about the sale. So it goes to show that it's always a classy and personal move that could mean the difference in winning the deal or not.

# 14

# Auction & Bank Owned Properties

Oftentimes online, you will see people or companies marketing homes that are foreclosures, pre-foreclosures, or short sales.

On the surface it can seem like a great deal. However, upon deeper investigation, it might or might not be as great of a deal as it might appear at first glance. One of the main differences is these properties are rarely move-in-ready.

If you are a first time homebuyer or don't have a large amount of money or experience repairing a property, getting into an old or foreclosed property that needs some TLC is often both costly and risky.

Anothing thing to consider if and when you're looking at foreclosures is the loan program you're going with. Certain loan programs have baseline requirements in terms of the condition that the property must be in to qualify for the loan. Be sure to tell your Loan Officer if you are thinking about making an offer on a foreclosed property or a short sale to ensure the property will meet the minimum requirements of the loan program you've chosen.

# 15

# What Credit Score Do I Need To Get A Mortgage?

The minimum required credit score you will need in order to qualify will depend on a number of factors, primarily including the loan program for which you are applying.

Generally speaking, government loan programs such as VA and FHA loans will take credit scores as low as 580. USDA loans usually require a score of 640 or higher. Conventional loans will have the highest requirements for credit scores, with their minimum requirements being in the ballpark of 660 or higher.

With that being said, at the time at which this book was written, Covid-19 has impacted many families and industries across the globe, including the housing and mortgage space. Due to many individuals being furloughed from their jobs or laid off completely, many Lenders across the country either temporarily or permanently increased their minimum qualifying scores.

So when it comes to credit score, just making the cut does not always guarantee an approval. The actual contents of your credit report will be weighed in making a determination on approval. For example, you might have a qualifying credit score of 620 but if you have multiple late payments in the last 12 months or all of your credit cards are maxed out, you're going to be seen as a high risk client to the bank from a Lending standpoint.

Another rule of thumb is the lower your credit score is, the higher your interest rate will be.

If your score only meets minimum qualifying requirements, you might also have to provide additional documentation such as proof that you have paid other bills on time for the last 12+ months (such as cell phone bill or utilities), or you might be required to show that you have at least 3 months or more worth of proposed mortgage payments in total assets, NOT including your down payment and closing costs. This can be a combination of checking, savings, retirement, investments, etc.

In summary, a credit score over 640 usually equates to more options for loan programs, lower interest rates, and a smoother process in general.

# 16

# What Will You Look At When I Apply For A Mortgage?

There are several factors that will be weighed and considered when purchasing a home from a Lending standpoint.

The first is your credit score and overall credit history which we just covered in the previous chapter. The second is your affordability.

I generally define affordability as your bills stacked against your income. Affordability is also defined by your "Debt to Income Ratio" or DTI. We want to see that you're not spending too much of your monthly income on debt alone. Most lenders want to see that your total DTI is no higher than 45%. FHA and VA loans have more lenient requirements on DTI than conventional loans.

We also look to see if you have any collections or judgements.

A lot of times there are unpaid collections or other accounts on a credit report that people don't realize that are there.

Maybe they have a collection that was from an old medical bill that they thought had been paid through insurance.

Many times there are collections that have already been paid or are inaccurate altogether. Your Loan Officer can usually recommend a licensed credit repair professional if you have dated or inaccurate information on your credit report that needs to be disputed and/or removed.

The Underwriter might require certain judgements or collections to be paid in full prior to granting final approval and clear to close. It will all depend on the nature, type, and amount owed on the specific judgement or collection.

The Underwriter will also look to see if you've had a bankruptcy in the last 7-10 years. Depending on the type of bankruptcy and the loan type you're trying to qualify for, you'll usually have to wait a minimum of 2-4 years from the date the bankruptcy was discharged and/or dismissed in order to qualify for a home loan.

All of the above mentioned factors will play a part in determining your loan approval so make sure you fully understand your credit profile and personal finances.

# 17

# What Does It Mean To Pre-Qualify For A Home Loan?

Oftentimes the term pre-approval and pre-qualification get used interchangeably. For this book, I will use my own definitions of each.

You can be pre-approved without being pre-qualified. If you apply for a pre-approval, have your credit pulled, but do not submit any other personal documents, your pre-approval is only as good as the information you put on the application which leaves a massive amount of room for error.

On the other hand, being pre-qualified means you have not only applied for a mortgage, but also had your Loan Officer pull your credit, review your financial documents including pay stubs, tax returns, bank statements, etc. etc. Once this happens, your Loan Officer will submit your file through an Automated Underwriting System (AUS) to determine whether or not you qualify for a home purchase, and furthermore what your options will be in terms of loan programs.

You should not feel comfortable beginning your home search unless you have been pre-qualified by a licensed Lender.

We want to make sure that your financial documents match what you indicated on the application.

Everything on your application gets verified and considered to see if it meets the guidelines for that particular program. This usually happens in the official Underwriting stage of the process.

Pre-qualified means we've actually gone in and looked at your financial documents and made sure that it all checks out.

# 18

# Minimum Down Payments

How much money you'll have to put down will depend almost entirely on the loan program.

When it comes to different loan options, each program's requirements for minimum down payment are pretty black and white.

As discussed in previous chapters, there are zero down payment options with the VA loan and USDA program.

If you don't qualify for a no down payment option, there are a number of low down payment products available such as an FHA purchase which requires 3.5% down.

Even Conventional loans now have programs to compete with the other more popular government programs.

For example, Fannie Mae offers a conventional program called Home Ready, that requires as low as 3% down. Similarly, Freddie Mac's Home Possible program also offers down payments as little as 3%. However, much like USDA loans, these 3% down options have income limits and minimum credit score requirements as well as tight limits on DTI.

Outside of those options are your traditional conventional loan products which have fewer requirements aside from credit score and caps on debt-to-income ratio. A traditional conventional loan will require somewhere between 5-20% down.

# 19

# Out Of Pocket Costs

Outside of your down payment, there are a couple costs that you'll need to be prepared to pay for out of pocket during the process. Some of these fees are rolled into the closing costs which can be paid for by the buyer, seller, lender, or a combination thereof.

The most common of costs include:

- Home appraisal
- Title fees
- Home inspections
- Pre-paid taxes or insurance
- Third party fees

You will receive a Loan Estimate when you apply for a home loan showing you all the costs associated with the mortgage company as well as the title company, both of which you have the right to choose.

# 20

# Should I Pay Discount Points?

You might be thinking "Hold up for a second... what's a discount point?" Before you get too excited, no, discount points don't mean you get a discount on your down payment, interest rate, or closing costs. As a matter of fact, it's quite the opposite.

Discount points refer to the cost you will pay for getting a lower interest rate with any given lender.

Many people think buying a discount or paying discount points will make a *big* difference in payment. This might or might not be true. In a market like the one we're in now where rates are at historic all time lows, buying down your rate only makes sense in rare cases.

A good way to figure out if it makes financial sense is to do a quick equation. But first, it's good to know that one discount point equates to 1% of the loan amount.

Let's say $2,000 in discount points lowers your interest rate by a half of a percentage point, which translates to lowering your payment by $50 per month. If you divide the cost for the lower rate by the amount you're saving (or in this case 2,000/50), you get 40. Meaning it will take you 40 months (or

3.3 years) to recoup the cost for the lower rate, which might not be worth it. However, if it's a property you plan to hold for the long term, maybe the savings over the life of the loan make more sense. Only you (and maybe your financial advisor) can decide which option is best for your specific financial goals.

Each person has a different financial profile, so that's why it's important to run a cost savings analysis to see if it makes sense to pay discount points. If you're still confused, ask your Loan Officer to help you figure out the total cost savings analysis.

The clearer you are on your financial goals, the easier it will be to determine if you should pay discount points or not.

But again, it's never been cheaper to borrow money than it is right now, so don't get too stuck on rate. It's likely your Mom or Dad had a rate of 6-8% on their first home which would have been considered fantastic at that time.

# 21

# The Difference Between A Fixed-Rate Mortgage And ARM Loan

A fixed rate mortgage is exactly what it sounds like. The rate is fixed and stays the same for the entire loan term. Nothing changes. So, if you have the loan for the full term of 10, 20, or 30 years the interest rate will not change unless you refinance for any given reason.

The only thing that might change your actual payment are your property taxes and homeowners insurance which sometimes increase over time or due to a myriad of different factors.

Now, on an ARM or Adjustable Rate Mortgage, the interest rate will adjust after the initial fixed period.

Depending on what ARM program you choose, your rate might go up or down depending on what the market is doing and what index the ARM is tied to. Without getting too technical, there are different indexes that are associated with different economic factors such as US treasuries. But even adjustable rate mortgages have caps to protect your rate from increasing to an unmanageable level.

In the current low rate environment that we are in, it's not usually going to make sense to go with an ARM. However, in markets where rates are higher, an ARM might make sense, particularly when you only plan on keeping the property for 5-7 years or less.

Each type of mortgage has its own pros and cons so it is very important that you speak with your lender and look at each type of loan to see what best fits for your unique situation.

# 22

# What Will My Mortgage Payment Include?

Your total mortgage payment is made up of the following: Principal, interest, tax and insurance.

We often abbreviate this as PITI.

Principal - The amount of the loan that you borrowed.

Interest- The percentage that the bank or institution charges for lending you the principle loan amount.

Tax- The taxes charged by the local and state governments. Taxes are based on the assessed value, which the city determines. This is why you always want your assessed value to be low and your appraised value to be high as the appraisal determines the actual *value* of the home... not the assessment which is a common misconception.

Insurance- The homeowners insurance (often referred to as hazard insurance) is to protect both you, the buyer, as well as the lender against any damage or problems with the property by insuring it.

# 23

# Can Someone Give Me Money For My Down Payment?

Absolutely! But there are rules that must be met if you are receiving money from somebody else for your down payment or closing costs.

When it comes to gift money, documentation is king. Let's say for example Mom agrees to give you $5,000 towards your down payment. You will be required to provide a paper trail showing the source of the funds (i.e. a copy of Mom's bank statement covering a full 30 day period that show the funds clearing her account). As well as an updated bank statement from you, the buyer, showing the funds being available in your account.

You will also both have to sign a letter stating that the money is a gift and not a personal loan.

This supporting documentation is key to ensuring that we understand exactly what those funds are for and that they are to be assigned to the down payment of the home.

# 24

# Owning V. Renting

While there is absolutely a time and a season for renting, in almost every single case, ownership will trump renting 10 out of 10 times.

On the surface level it might seem like a gigantic pain in the rear end to spend a notable amount of time and money to find the right agent, home, and lender, when you can rent a house, apartment, or condo with one application and a security deposit.

But here's the rub... When you pay rent every month, you're paying your Landlord's mortgage. Additionally, even though your Landlord's mortgage is fixed, your rent is not.

Rent increases by an average of 3%-5% annually, nationwide. So you usually end up paying just as much if you were to have purchased a home, just spread out over a longer period of time, and with nothing to show for it.

Once you own a home, you're not just a homeowner. You're an asset owner. And that asset that you now manage and own will appreciate in value year over year. That asset will provide you with passive wealth that you can tap into if and when you need it. This passive wealth is also referred to as equity.

There are also tax breaks involved so you're able to write certain things off when tax season rolls around.

You can't really write anything off when you rent. If there's stuff that you've bought to fix up the house you're renting, you can't write that kind of stuff off on taxes in most cases.

Lastly, owning your own home triggers a big mindset shift. This is something that is rarely talked about when comparing renting to owning. But it's worth discussing.

When you accomplish a goal like homeownership, you are sending a powerful message to your subconscious that you have the power and ability to achieve so much more. Oftentimes homeownership is the starting point for people that results in a domino effect in terms of crushing other life goals. This was my personal experience, as well as that of many of my clients.

# 25

# How Long Does It Take To Buy A House?

Usually it takes 30 to 45 days from the time you have a ratified purchase contract on a property until you close.

There could be some circumstances that come up that might delay the process for one party or the other, but that is the most common timeline generally speaking.

For example, if you purchase a short sale home it might take 3 months to get approval from the bank, and furthermore to get to closing. If you're dealing with a bank owned property, plan on 60+ days for sure.

The timeline will also depend on the turn times of third parties involved such as the appraiser, Underwriting department, Title company, etc.

With this being said, once you are under contract, the clock begins ticking, and you could be considered in breach of contract if you do not provide the required documentation to your Loan Officer in a timely manner. So be sure to make communication with your Loan Officer a top priority once your offer has been accepted.

# 26

# What Is An Earnest Money Deposit?

Earnest money is the money you put in up front in trust to show the seller you are serious about the offer.

The money is held in what's called an escrow account and is credited back to you, the buyer, at closing.

Often, sellers want to know they are not wasting their time with potential buyers. So, an earnest money deposit is given to show good faith that the potential buyer is serious about purchasing the home. In our market, the most common amount for an earnest money deposit is $500.

Once your offer is accepted, your earnest money check will be held in house at the title company you've chosen for settlement and closing. These funds will then be credited back to you at closing in the form of being deducted from your total closing costs. If your closing costs are covered in full by the seller, you are refunded the amount of your earnest money deposit at closing.

# 27

# Is There A Loan Program That Allows Me To Fix Up A House In Need Of Repairs?

So you found a house in the right location, that's the right size, and is even under budget! The only problem is it looks like something out of a Real Estate Horror Story blog. *cue scream sound bite*

There are ways in which you can wrap in the cost to rehab a property into the loan itself. The most common of programs that allow this is the FHA 203K Loan.

There are two types of 203k loans. A Limited 203k and a Standard 203k. A limited 203k is a more streamlined version, and is primarily for cosmetic repairs. The amount of repairs on a limited 203k loan may not exceed $35,000.

A standard 203k is designed for a full rehab in which you are either gutting the home and/or adding to the physical structure of the property.

Both options allow you to finance both the purchase price of the property as well as repairs all in one.

For example, let's say you find a home priced at $150,000, but it's determined that the home needs about $50,000 worth of repairs. Your total base loan amount would then be $193,000 (purchase price, plus improvements, minus down payment).

Although it might seem like a great option, this program comes with it's own set of challenges and requirements. Spoiler alert… Buckle up for a complex and convoluted process. Some Loan Officers are required to have additional certifications in Rehab Loans in order to offer them to their clients. Be sure to have a thorough and detailed conversation with your Loan Officer about what the 203k process looks like before committing to go that route.

# 28

# Is There A Difference Between Buying A Home To Live In And Buying An Investment Property?

There's not only a difference, there is a big difference. When buying a home to live in, you are purchasing what is called a primary residence. A primary residence purchase affords you with the option of little to no money down (based on what you qualify for).

Purchasing an investment property on the other hand is when you buy a home with the intention of renting it out... When you're buying an investment property obviously it's in the name itself. It's an investment, which requires a little (or a lot) more money down. Generally, investment homes require at least 20% down. Not all loan programs allow you to purchase an investment property either. Generally speaking, investment property purchases are going to be almost 100% conventional.

Aside from the purpose of the home, the biggest difference is going to be in the interest rate and therefore your overall cash due at closing. Qualifying for an investment property might not be as easy compared to qualifying for a primary residence purchase.

# 29

# Four Questions To Ask When Buying A Flip

You've seen the eye grabbing pictures online; The beautiful furniture, the open floor plan, quartz, stainless steel appliances.. It's all new! *cue eye heart emojis*

A home is considered 'flipped' when an investor buys a home in need of repairs, strips it down and remodels the entire property, and sells or "flips" it for a profit. Sometimes they even install new landscaping and other outdoor features.

First time buyers especially love these flipped homes. Sure, it's gorgeous on the surface level, but there are critical things to be aware of when purchasing a flip.

Here are four questions you should ask before closing on this beauty.

## What is the home's history?

Everything is public record now, so ask your Realtor for the transaction history. This can be found on the city or county website under assessment history. Why? This will show when the investor bought the home and how much they paid for it. It will also show the square footage, bedroom and bath count.

An investor might take a patio and create a bedroom or add a shower or even a full bathroom. What has been done to the property is key because it will tell you how extensive the remodel was and what was involved.

As the buyer, you want to know if there's been any plumbing or electrical moved around or added.

### Are there any improvements?

Ask the seller for a list of improvements and request them to document it. You want to know where those appliances came from as well.

This will help you during the inspection period. Especially pay attention to any electrical and plumbing that's been moved, altered or added.

### Can you use your inspector?

Just because a home has been flipped, doesn't mean that it was done to top notch standards. You will want to have a reputable licensed Home Inspector complete the inspection to ensure that no corners were cut and everything was done up to code.

I would also advise getting a lateral sewer inspection and have a licensed electrician check the panels. Lots of flippers add more electrical outlets, microwaves and other appliances without upgrading the panel. This is a possible fire hazard and will be expensive to upgrade later.

## Where are the permits?

Lots of remodeled homes may have additions without permits. It is not necessarily always required, but any additions should be done in a workmanship like manner, and a permit can help confirm this.

If not, the lender may have issues when the appraisal is done. Ask the seller for the name and license number of the contractor that did the work in case the appraisal requires them to provide additional supporting documentation.

If you have issues later, you have recourse against the contractor. It's a red flag if the work is not done by a licensed contractor. Even better if they have their Class A status.

With that being said, flips can also make for wonderful homes with lots of new upgrades without building from the ground up. You just want to make sure you do your homework before settling on this kind of transaction.

# 30

# Condos Are An Affordable Path To Homeownership

Condominiums and townhomes are a great way to enter the homeownership market.

They are typically more affordable in terms of purchase price and require less maintenance from you, the homeowner.

The right complex will appreciate in value as much as a single family neighborhood. With recent finance changes, condominiums are easier to finance too than they used to be. However, not all condos are approved for FHA or VA financing, so if you know you're getting either an FHA or VA loan, you'll want to ensure that the condo association is VA and FHA approved prior to going to look at the property. Your Lender can verify this information for you.

Most buyers who cannot afford a single family home will say "I'll continue to rent, I don't want to pay HOA dues, they are a waste of money!".

I then ask, "Do you know what the HOA fee covers?"

Compared to the cost and maintenance of a single family home, HOA's can be a bargain!

Let's look at how this saves you money –

|  | **Single Family Home** | **Condo/HOA** |
|---|---|---|
| Water Bill | $100 | $50 |
| Gardener | $50 | $0 |
| Trash/Sewer | $50 | $0 |
| Insurance | $100 | $50 |
| Maintenance | $75 | $0 |
| Total | $475 | $100 |
| Pool | $250 | $0 |
| Total | $725 | $100 |
| HOA | $0 | $350 |

*Costs can vary. These costs are an estimate from a typical Southern California home.

In this example, a $350 HOA fee covers $725 in costs/expenses if you have a pool.

Condominiums and townhomes are an excellent way to start investing in real estate.

You're in control of the interior and the exterior is maintained by the HOA.

Many buyers purchase a single family home and become overwhelmed with the upkeep and maintenance. Buying a home with an HOA also frees up your time.

Owning a condo compared to renting? There is no comparison! With ownership, you gain appreciation, equity, tax advantages and the peace of mind of knowing your payment is fixed for 15 or 30 years depending on your loan term.

It's truly the only way to control your long term housing expenses.

# 31

# What Are Contingencies?

Contingencies are essentially the specific terms of a purchase contract that must be met by one or both parties in order for the contract to be considered binding.

Any given purchase contract will have a number of varying contingencies, but there are 3 primary contingencies you need to pay close attention to.

If you miss one, you could be considered to be in breach of contract in which the seller can technically deem the contract to be null and void, and sell the home to someone else.

An experienced agent and lender will know the meaning of all of the contingencies and will make sure you understand them, as well as keep everyone on the appropriate timeline.

The first main contingency is the **property inspection**.

The seller usually gives you between 5-15 days to order inspections needed in order to be satisfied with the condition of the property.

This is the time you verify the roof doesn't leak, the sewers drain, the electrical systems are adequate, and further research any red flags that these inspections uncover.

Your agent will go back to the seller and will either accept the property as is or ask for repairs or further negotiations.

The second main contingency is the **appraisal**.

As discussed in previous chapters, your lender will order the appraisal at either the same time as the home inspection, or just after the home inspection is received. The appraiser usually has about 17 days or less to complete the appraisal report, however in high volume market conditions, you might see longer turn times on appraisals as well as other steps in the process.

Once received, the Lender will review the appraisal, verify it came in at at least the sales price and requires no repairs.

The third and biggest contingency is the **loan contingency**.

By meeting this contingency, it means your loan has been fully reviewed by an Underwriter who has issued a formal loan approval and commitment.

In this very competitive seller's market, being choosy about your contingencies is a great way to make your offer better than others, without paying a higher price.

The less contingencies there are, typically the quicker the process will move, and the more attractive the offer will be to the seller. But the nature of contingencies is to protect both parties, so be calculated about which contingencies you remove and add.

In rare cases, a buyer might choose to write a contract with no contingencies, also known as buying the home "as is", making the buyer all but equal to a cash buyer aside from formal financing.

You might be wondering 'how do we do that?'. We fully underwrite and pre-approve the buyer BEFORE the offer is accepted. Most lenders call this a TBD approval. They essentially review all of your income and asset documents and issue a loan approval contingent on only title work, appraisal, and a ratified purchase contract.

# 32

# Explore Your Down Payment Options

When buying a home, you will need to have funds set aside for different expenses. These expenses are broken into three categories: down payment, closing costs, and up front expenses (such as your earnest money deposit, home inspection, and appraisal (which some lenders wrap into the closing costs).

In general, closing costs will make up about 3% of the sales price. Your down payment of course will depend on the loan program you have chosen. Many closing costs are fixed costs and aren't dependent on purchase price, so the lower the purchase price, the higher percentage you'll need to ask the sellers for if you want all of your closing costs covered. 3% of $150,000 is very different from 3% of $400,000.

If you're using VA home loan benefits, you will not need a down payment, otherwise, consider these options.

You might be one of many first time home buyers who don't have a ton of cash available for a down payment and closing costs. Luckily, there are some creative ways to come up with the required funds needed depending on your personal situation.

Let's explore a few options...

## 401K Loan –

If you have a 401K, TSP or other retirement account, you should ask the plan administrator if you can take out a loan. Most plans allow you to borrow up to 50% of the balance. You might even be able to set the interest rate and payment.

It is not a taxable event because it's not a withdrawal. Instead, you are borrowing the money from yourself. The lender will not count the payment against you and lower your approval amount.

IRA's do not usually allow for a loan and can only be a withdrawal. Be sure to ask your financial advisor or a CPA about the tax repercussions of this.

## Down Payment Grants –

Grants are available through cities, counties and states. In most cases, grants do not have to be repaid, but be sure to read the fine print of any grant funds to ensure there are no minimum requirements of how long you must own the property for, or other contingencies.

Most grants will cover a portion of the downpayment and or closing costs. These types of programs can be a great way to buy a home if you don't have the funds yourself.

## Lender Credits –

Technically, you cannot use lender credits for a down payment. You can, however, use the credits for closing costs, saving your cash for the down payment.

How does a Lender credit work?

A lender credit is when you opt for a higher interest rate in exchange for your lender covering a portion of your closing costs. You will need to look at all interest rate options to see if the higher rate is worth the extra cash at closing.

For example… Your options for interest rates might include a rate of 3.5% with no lender credit and no fee/discount points. This would be considered "par".

Let's then say the seller is only willing to contribute $3,000 towards closing costs, but you need about $5,000 to have all of your costs covered. The Lender might offer a rate of 4.25% in exchange for a lender credit of $2,000 to help cover that spread. But be sure the higher rate still keeps you within your budget in terms of your monthly payment.

## Gift Funds –

You might be fortunate enough to have a sweet Aunt Lola who loves you so much that she's willing to give you the funds you need for down payment and closing costs. This is actually totally permissible. Your lender will consider this money as "gift funds".

As discussed in previous chapters, there are very specific requirements for how gift funds must be documented and sourced.

The lender will ask for a copy of the donor's bank statement and a letter stating this money does not have to be repaid which both parties will sign.

## Borrow From an Asset –

You can also borrow money from an existing asset, but only if you can afford another payment in your debt ratio and still qualify for your desired purchase price.

Many buyers can refinance their car if it's owned free and clear. (although a car is not usually considered a true asset). Or if you own another property, you might be able to pull some cash out of the equity you have in the form of a home equity line of credit.

Guidelines and requirements in the Mortgage space are ever changing, so make sure you speak with an experienced loan officer who clearly outlines the options available to you and who can create a financing package that helps you meet your real estate goals.

# 33

# Let's Talk About Sewers

Waste and sewers are also a topic of importance in the home purchase process. You'll need to know what kind of sewer system the home is connected to.

There are basically two types. A public sewer takes all the waste water from your home into the main sewer pipes under the street.

If you live in a rural area where no public sewer is available, you will have a septic tank. This is a giant tank buried in your yard where the wastewater goes and must be pumped out occasionally.

Today we're talking about public sewers which are most common.

When purchasing a home, a lateral sewer inspection is highly recommended. During the inspection phase of your purchase, you can contract a licensed plumber to send a camera down through the main drain.

The camera will show, through a video, exactly what is clear or blocked all the way to the main sewer line in the street.

Remember when we discussed pitfalls of buying a flip? This is one area that can be a particularly big problem when buying an investor remodeled home or a flip.

Unfortunately, some flippers give flipped homes a bad reputation due to cutting corners.

For example, a lazy flipper might demo a home without bothering to cover the hole where the toilet once went. All of that construction debris can clog up the pipes. They then might set a new toilet there without bothering to verify that the drains are clear.

It might seem like a small oversight, but it becomes a problem when all of a sudden the drainage system gets severely backed up one day. This might result in having to call a plumber to come out which can get costly (and smelly) very quickly.

A normal property inspection does not discover this problem which is why flips are seen as a higher level of risk to the buyer. But don't let that deter you too much. There are lots of very professional and reputable investors who treat their flips as if they were to live there themselves. Your Realtor or Lender will probably know a few good ones and can warn you of others.

Another main reason for sewage backups are tree roots.

When the inspection camera goes through the line, you will be able to see all the dirt, cracks and roots that can block the main line. Since it's lateral, it does not really drain downhill and can easily clog with debris. This is the time you would show the video to the seller and request repairs or renegotiate a change satisfactory to both parties.

Don't find yourself on the wrong end of a clogged drain. Get an inspection.

# 34

# Attention Military - Top 5 Reasons You Want To Use Your VA Loan Benefit

First of all, if you've served our country or are currently serving, thank you for your truly noble sacrifice. Your bravery and service are recognized and appreciated.

If you have served or are currently serving, you likely qualify for the VA home loan. This is one amazing benefit of your service that you absolutely should take advantage of.

VA loans offer no down payment, lower rates, no mortgage insurance and generous underwriting guidelines.

Let's look at the top 5 reasons you should use your VA home loan benefit.

## No Down Payment –

The new national conforming loan limit is now $548,250.

This means anywhere in the country, you can buy a home using VA financing with zero money down.

In high cost counties, mostly metropolitan areas, the max loan amount can be higher.

## No PMI –

Unless you bring in 20% cash down payment, your lender will require you to have Private Mortgage Insurance to protect them in case of a foreclosure.

Not with VA!

The VA loan program is paid for with a funding fee, a one time cost added to the loan. If you have at least a 10% service related disability, this fee will be waived entirely. If you are using your VA eligibility for the first time, the VA funding fee is 2.3% of the purchase price and is rolled into the loan itself. The funding fee is increased for subsequent use of the VA loan.

This saves the average home buyer $150-500 a month on the payment.

## Generous Credit Guidelines –

VA loans are the only home loans that allow you to buy a home two years following a major derogatory event like bankruptcy, foreclosure and short sale. Although, if any of those apply to you, you might be required to provide additional documentation to show a good record of money management and ontime payments post bankruptcy.

They also allow much lower credit scores than other loan programs.

## Qualify For a Higher Loan Amount –

There is also a higher threshold on debt to income ratios with the VA loan. This benefits most military buyers in allowing them to qualify for substantially more than with other programs.

## Better Interest Rates –

VA loans usually carry a lower interest rate than other programs.

Keep in mind that the rule of thumb with interest rates and credit scores is the higher the score, the lower the rate and vice versa -- the lower the score, the higher the rate. This applies to the VA loan as well.

If your score is in the high 500's to low 600's, you are better off taking a few months to improve your credit score before buying. It will likely save you big time in interest.

VA loans can also be used more than once, and in some cases, you can have more than one VA loan at a time.

Your best bet is to talk to an experienced VA lender who can share their knowledge who can recommend an experienced agent if you don't have one already.

The teamwork of a good agent/lender will ensure your offer gets accepted, your timelines met and have you moving into your home on time.

# 35

# 15 Year Mortgage vs 30 Year Mortgage

Many times throughout the week I get asked, "Is it better to do a 15 or a 30 year mortgage"?

So, the question I ask in return is, "What are you trying to accomplish by getting a 15-year loan versus a 30-year loan"?

Most of the time the answer to this question is that they just want to pay the loan off quicker than 30 years.

This is one area in which I will offer up an opinion. But it's just that, an opinion. Every person has their own unique situation and financial goals, so no part of the home purchase process is 'one size fits all', including the loan term.

Historically speaking, a 15 year made sense for some due to the fact that the rates were much lower and the duration of the loan much shorter. However, in what is now a record breaking market, interest rates on 30 year mortgages now beat what 15 year rates looked like years ago. Thanks, CoronaVirus!

So by that logic, it's never been cheaper to borrow money to buy a home specifically. Personally, I would opt for the lower payment (AKA the 30 year mortgage), and would use the additional cash flow monthly to invest, or pay down other higher interest debt. I'll bust out an example in just a couple paragraphs.

A quick Google search of a few calculators can easily answer if the 15 year makes more financial sense. Which brings a good point to reiterate that getting ultra clear on your goals is absolutely essential during the home purchase process.

So let's break it down now... *cue disco rif*

The first Google search I run is for a mortgage calculator. For our example today, we are going to keep it simple. No need to go full Elon Musk on this.

We will use a loan amount of $250,000 with a 4% interest rate for a 30-year note and a 3.75% interest rate for a 15-year note.

*This is just an example and not a guarantee that either of these interest rates are attainable at the time of reading this book.*

If we take the $250,000 loan amount with these interest rates, we will quickly determine that the principal and interest payment for the 30-year note is $1,194, and the payment for the 15-year note is $1,818, a monthly difference of $624.

The second piece we need Google to help us with is an investment calculator. I am not guaranteeing any rate on return from any investment. Again, this is just for example purposes.

Google quickly found me an investment calculator because it's awesome like that. I entered in our $624 monthly difference for 15 years, which is the time difference between the 30-year note and the 15-year note.

I used an average interest rate of 6%. (Most will agree, this is an extremely conservative figure for rate of return.) After 15 years of investing that extra cash at this ROI, I determined I would have $175,785.91 in my investment account. *cue shake your money maker.*

Not too shabby, right?

The final Google search led me to my amortization schedule.

Guess what it showed me?

After 15 years of paying my minimum monthly payment my balance is $161,357. I could write a check, from that investment account, for the entire amount and still have over $14,000 left over.

The financially disciplined borrower can take the difference and invest it into a non-qualified, diversified, mutual fund account with a good financial coach and have access to the money if and when they need it.

Signing the 30-year note will allow you to build up some additional wealth and should something happen, you now have access to the funds needed to do unforeseen repairs or cover unexpected life event expenses.

In the event you already have a sizable non-qualified account to pull from maybe the 15-year mortgage is the best way to go. Only you and your trusted financial advisor can determine which is best.

# 36

# More Money Down Or Nah?

A couple times a month I will get asked questions about putting more money down on a home on top of the minimum requirement.

Usually this is a situation where a borrower has either saved up money specifically because someone told them they must put 20% down, or they really just don't want PMI (private mortgage insurance).

Sometimes this question comes up because someone wants to close out an old retirement account and utilize that money for a down payment.

I like to utilize a combination of math and financial wisdom to see how best to advise a borrower.

Let's pretend that you have saved up $50,000 for your down payment, because you thought you needed that much.

That would provide for you a $250,000 sales price on your home ($50,000 = 20% of $250,000).

Using a quick Google search to develop a base, I started with a $200,000 loan amount with a 4% interest rate and a 30-year mortgage.

That quickly shows us that a monthly payment for principal and interest would be $955 per month.

The next calculation I used was on a $241,250 loan amount, using an FHA 3.5% minimum down payment.

Our payment is now $197 **more** per month.

The answer to whether the borrower should invest the extra money depends on their whole financial picture.

If you took that same $41,250 and put it in a shoebox under your bed, each month you could go grab the extra $197 to pay your mortgage payment and you would have money in that shoe box for over 209 months. That translates to over 17 years!

Using that same Google investment calculator, we can see that if we averaged a 3% rate of return on that $41,250, we would end up with $68,179.96 after those same 17 years. Furthermore, if we left it alone for the full 30 years that we pay on our mortgage, we would have over $100,000!

But remember, mortgage insurance never falls off on FHA loans, regardless of the amount of equity you have. You have it for the life of the loan unless you refinance. So if you have good credit and are able to put 5% or more down, Conventional loans are usually the better option. If not, FHA is still a wonderful loan program and is what I used to purchase my first home.

When figuring out how far your down payment money will go, a good rule of thumb is to realize that on average you will only save about $5 per month for every $1,000 that you put down on the mortgage.

Is it worth saving $5 per month?

The answer is completely up to you, the borrower.

I have had many people put the extra money down because they had saved the money for this specific purpose and they know their monthly budget will allow the payment at the lower amount. That's cool! You do you.

They usually fear that if they choose to keep the money they will spend it on something else and their monthly budget will be out of tune.

I have also had many families decide to use that money to start an investment account with a local financial advisor and treat the purchase of their home like an investment tool.

## 37

# Do You Like To Gamble?

Throughout each month I am probably asked a million times, "Well what are interest rates right now?"

Here is the amusing piece to that question, if I were to ask someone what the interest rate on their home is currently, 80% have no idea!

This is only a question that matters when financing the home.

So naturally my follow up question is usually, "What would you like it to be?"... Because here is the big secret of interest rates... Are you ready?

Your interest rate can be as low as the amount you're willing to pay for it. Plain and simple.

On a higher level, rates are determined primarily by the Bond market... More specifically, mortgage backed securities. So when bond prices go up and down based on the appetite of investors across the country, rates will fluctuate accordingly.

There are other economic factors that determine rates as well such as inflation, unemployment rate, etc. At the time at which this book was written, rates are at historic lows due to the Fed manipulating the bond market by purchasing billions in mortgage backed securities weekly. This is driving interest rates down which is needed in a national pandemic where folks are hurting to pay their bills. This could be seen as one of the silver linings of Covid-19.

Our local market is pretty competitive and most mortgage bankers in this area have virtually the same rates, so shopping for an interest rate usually doesn't make up for the time spent shopping.

I often tell my clients that cheapest is almost never best. If you shop long and hard enough, you'll almost always find a lower rate than the last guy. But be prepared to sacrifice in other critical pieces of the transaction such as communication, responsiveness, transparency, and trust regarding fees and costs.

Here is where I let, you, the borrower make a choice.

We can look at rates all the way down to the lower 2% range.

That only means if you want that rate, you need to know how much you are willing to pay for it. If the lower rate would save you $100/month on your payment, and costs you $2,000 (in discount points), it will take you 20 months to recoup the cost (2,000/100). So a quick math equation can help you determine if it's worth it to you.

Let's do another example using more specific figures. We found a perfect home for $235,000. We will utilize a 3.5% down payment program to give us a loan amount of $226,775 ($235,000 − 3.5% ($8,225) = $226,775)

A quick jump to our handy dandy Google calculator will show you that the difference between a 4.25% and 4.125% is between $16 and $17 per month.

Let's make an assumption that for every 1/8 of an interest rate (.125%) the fee is half of a point or .5%.

So for our scenario a 4.25% interest rate would cost you $0 in discount points, but for a 4.125% (an 1/8 difference) it would cost you half a point, or $1,133.87.

Are you with me so far?

Now we need to determine how many months of saving our $16-$17 per month it will take to recover the initial cost.

So for our mathematicians out there, we take the difference in payment from the original payment to the new payment ($,1116-$1,099 = $17).

Then we divide that into the cost of the buy down to determine months to make up payment ($1,133.88 / $17 = 66.70).

So, for us to invest $1,133.88 up front it would take us 66.70 months or just over 5.5 years.

This brings me back around to my original question: Do you like to gamble? Will you be in this same house for more than 5.5 years?

Here is a quick table of what the fee would be to "buy down" the interest rate and the number of months it would take to recover that fee based on our example:

*This is not a guarantee of what the discount fees cost, this is just an example.

| Loan Amount | | $226,775 | | |
|---|---|---|---|---|
| rate | price | cost | payment | month to make up payment |
| 4.250% | 0 | $ - | $1,116 | 0.00 |
| 4.125% | 0.5% | $1,133.88 | $1,099 | 66.70 |
| 4.000% | 1% | $2,267.75 | $1,083 | 68.72 |
| 3.875% | 1.5% | $3,401.63 | $1,066 | 68.03 |
| 3.750% | 2% | $4,535.50 | $1,050 | 68.72 |
| 3.625% | 2.5% | $5,669.38 | $1,034 | 69.14 |
| 3.500% | 3% | $6,803.25 | $1,018 | 69.42 |

# 38

# How Can I Best Be Prepared To Get A Home Loan

So we've covered the logistics of the home purchase process. Now we need to go over the DOs and DON'Ts, or as I like to call them, The 10 Commandments of Home Buying. This is a very resourceful tool to anyone looking to get ready to buy a home.

Breaking any of the following Commandments will likely result in the harsh consequence of the loan approval falling through. And nobody wants that to happen.

Here they are:

1. Thou shalt not change jobs, become self-employed or quit your job.

2. Thou shalt not finance a vehicle. You probably shouldn't be living in one either.

3. Thou shalt not use credit cards excessively or miss any other payments on any other accounts.

4. Thou shalt not spend money you have set aside for closing costs. No, not even on that sweet potato launcher.

5. Thou shalt not omit debts or liabilities from your loan application. Lying isn't a good look.

6. Thou shalt not buy furniture on credit or open up any new lines of credit.

7. Thou shalt not originate any additional inquiries on your credit

8. Thou shalt not make large deposits without checking with your Loan Officer first.

9. Thou shalt not change bank accounts.

10. Thou shalt not co-sign for a loan with anyone or for anyone or anything.

I think some of these are fairly obvious in terms of why you shouldn't do them, but let's dive deeper into the "why" behind each one...

1. Thou shalt not change jobs, become self-employed or quit your job.

   Most loan programs require a minimum of 30 days on a job, as long as you have been in that same line of employment, or education for that position before you can get a loan. The longer you have been employed in the same line of work the stronger the file. If you jump to self-employment, you need 2 years' worth of tax returns to verify income. And remember, when self employed, we can't the vast majority of your right offs towards your qualifying income.

2. Thou shalt not finance a vehicle.

   Not only will this drop your credit score due to the number of auto loan inquiries, but it could also increase your payment on this liability and knock you out of being able to qualify for your target price point.

3. Thou shalt no use credit cards excessively or miss any payments on any other accounts.

   Before closing, and all throughout the loan process, your credit is being monitored. The underwriting team will always do a soft pull credit report to insure debts, and monthly obligations have not increased. So don't pull a fast one.

4. Thou shalt not spend money you have set aside for closing costs.

   The loan officer will turn in bank statements to show stability in your savings account(s) and proof of funds to close. If you spend that money you can rest assured that your loan will not close on time or maybe at all.

5. Thou shalt not omit debts or liabilities from your loan application.

   This is basically lying about debts. If you omit them, when the debt is discovered, the underwriting team will question why it was omitted and the loan process might start over.

6. Thou shalt not buy furniture on credit or open up any new lines of credit.

   Just wait until you close on the house to furnish it if you're planning on financing it. Most of the time this is done because you get such a great deal and save 10% by purchasing today. When shopping for new furniture, just tell the salesperson, "I am closing on my house in a few weeks and cannot buy today, I am just looking." And whatever they tell you, do NOT let them run your credit.

7. Thou shalt not originate any additional inquiries on your credit.

    New inquiries on credit makes underwriters think there is new debt and will need to be explained by you in writing.

8. Thou shalt not make large deposits without checking with your Loan Officer first.

    Large deposits are not always suspicious but they will always need to be explained and in most cases, sourced if you want to count them towards your total assets. Check with your loan officer to see what the definition of a large deposit is on the loan program you are using for your home purchase. And what types of deposits can and can't be counted.

9. Thou shalt not change bank accounts.

    Why would you want to change banks in the middle of the largest financial transaction of your life? If you hate your current bank that much, change after we close on your new home.

10. Thou shalt not co-sign for a loan with anyone.

Co-signing on a loan now makes you liable for that loan as well. So now we must start over with this new debt on your application.

# 39

# Conclusion

So there you have it, folks! Now you're fully equipped and ready to go out and crush your real estate goals with confidence! By starting with education, you are providing yourself with a great benefit and upper hand in turning your dreams into reality.

My hope is that this book provided you with something you didn't know before and that you leave feeling empowered and encouraged.

## Are You Ready To Get Started?

### Reach out and let's chat...

Alexa Rae Faithful (NMLS #1465347)
706-338-5073
alexa@cmsmortgage.com
1612 Centerville Turnpike, Suite 307
Virginia Beach, VA 23464
Equal Housing Lender

www.ingramcontent.com/pod-product-compliance
Lightning Source LLC
Chambersburg PA
CBHW070659220526
45466CB00001B/502